Pura Vida Tail book #1

Lucky Little Sloth!

The true story of **Guanabana** the rescued baby sloth

Dirk Morgan with Lori Morgan

 Guanabana pronounced Gwaa-NAA-buh-nuh

Archway Publishing books may be ordered through booksellers or by contacting:

Archway Publishing
1663 Liberty Drive
Bloomington, IN 47403
www.archwaypublishing.com
844-669-3957

ISBN: 978-1-6657-3510-0 (sc)
ISBN: 978-1-6657-3511-7 (hc)
ISBN: 978-1-6657-3509-4 (e)

Print information available on the last page.

Archway Publishing rev. date: 03/22/2023

Preface

This serendipitous tale of a rescued baby sloth was originally titled *Guanabana, A Lucky Little Sloth*. It is a true story of the baby two-toed sloth we found and rescued in January of 2018 off a tropical beach near our jungle lodge on the Osa Peninsula in Costa Rica. The pitiful baby sloth created a worldwide sensation through social media and the news. It was reported by hundreds of news stations, magazines, and internet sites including National Geographic. Even the US ambassador to Costa Rica used the story of Guanabana to show the goodwill of Americans living in Costa Rica.

This lucky little sloth touched millions of hearts globally, and Lori and I wanted to retell the story in a book for children, adults, and all who love animals and nature. We drafted the story by candlelight that very same evening of the rescue. Unfortunately, a week later that notebook, along with all our possessions we had, were lost in a devastating fire that destroyed our beloved family Jungle home. Over a year passed, and our world was reeling from the COVID pandemic, so during lockdown, we began again the recounting of this story.

We have other stories of nature and wildlife encounters to tell. *Lucky Little Sloth* is the first book in our Pura Vida Tails collection. We hope you enjoy this story, as much as we enjoyed writing it

Introduction from the Authors

This first Pura Vida Tail takes place in a green, clean land still largely unspoiled by man. The Osa Peninsula in southern Costa Rica is home to Corcovado National Park, one of the most biodiverse areas left on our planet. It is protected for the preservation of both plants and animals. Here the lush green jungle meets the blue waters of the Pacific Ocean. The air is fresh and alive with the sights, sounds, and smells of the rainforest and its many creatures. At night, the sky is bejeweled with countless stars, undimmed by city lights.

The Osa Peninsula is a magical, rejuvenating, and healing land. It is home to countless rare and endangered creatures, large and small, many yet to be discovered! All rainforests are precious jewels of the earth, the lungs of our planet that breathe fresh, clean oxygenated air to us all. But they need our help! We must respect and cherish them by protecting and preserving them. The Osa rainforest is Earths gift to us. It is our responsibility then for us to pass that gift forward for future generations to appreciate and enjoy.

Acknowledgments

June and Bob Morgan were explorers and early conservationists. Their love of rivers and passion for expeditions into wild areas helped turn on and connect their family, friends, and thousands of guests to the wild, fragile beauty of places like Canada, West Virginia, and Costa Rica! They showed us all how to enjoy nature by "preservation through utilization"—that to appreciate, protect, and preserve the wilderness left to us, we must enjoy it wisely and sustainably. Their love and knowledge of nature is their legacy passed on to those who knew them.

Dedication

To our own legacy, our grandchildren, Evan, Rowan, Everlyn, Penny, June, Callen, Hugh, Scottie, Sophia and those gifts yet to arrive. Always leave a place for nature in your heart! With love and Pura Vida! Your G-pa and Nana

Dirk Morgan, Thane Maynard, Lori Morgan with Moe, the two-toed sloth above.

Foreword by Thane Maynard

The real-life adventure of saving a "lucky little sloth" in Costa Rica is a hopeful tale for animal lovers of any age. Wildlife all over the world faces lots of challenges today, but when people get involved and help animals, it proves that we can all thrive together. Lori and Dirk Morgan have explored wild areas from Ohio to Costa Rica all their lives and are the perfect authors to tell stories that help everyone fall in love with nature and its wild creatures.

—Thane Maynard, Director of Cincinnati Zoo and Botanical Gardens

CHAPTER 1

A Land of Pura Vida

The warm, tropical morning began as a brilliant flash of orange, red, and yellow flooded the eastern sky. With a bright burst, the sun spiked through the distant, dark mountains and volcanoes far beyond the calm waters of the Golfo Dulce.

Golfo dulce means "sweet gulf" in Spanish. In times of heavy rains, the many freshwater streams flowing into it can form what's called a sweet, a less salty layer on top of the gulf's surface.

Brown pelicans perched high in the treetops saw it first, as they stretched and opened their wings wide to capture the first warm rays of the dawn. Soon they would join other sea birds—frigates, gulls, cormorants, and terns—hunting for their morning meal in the warm shallows of the blue water below.

Sunshine twinkled magically on the gentle wave tops, traveling beyond the waters and into the jungle. Golden sunbeams reached the gulf's far green shore, piercing the lush darkness and illuminating the dense rainforest with pinpoints of light, highlighting every shade of green imaginable.

In the jungle, among the branches of a humongous Ficus tree, a small troop of black howler monkeys had been up before dawn's first light. The big male of the troop announced the new day with a deep, low growl that grew louder and thundered over the vast jungle with a mighty roar. The other howler monkeys sat quietly, listening intently for a reply from distant howler monkeys in the area.

Howler monkeys, although small, are the loudest mammals on earth. Their call can be heard up to five miles away. In this manner, they communicate to one another where their troop is so they may keep their distance from other troops.

A flock of green parrots awoke, and with a screech, burst forth into the air from the treetops as countless insects—chirping, buzzing, flying, creeping, and crawling—began singing their joyful morning songs at once. The Osa Peninsula rainforest was awakening, and its sleepy creatures rose to another picture-perfect day in paradise. A troop of white-faced monkeys was at home in the tall coconut treetops. A Mama monkey yawned and stretched as she kept a wary eye on her young playing and chattering away in jabbery monkey talk. They leaped joyfully from limb to limb, chasing one other, playing keep-away with a small green coconut.

White-faced or capuchin monkeys love to eat the fresh meat and drink the water of the tender green coconuts. In times of food shortage, they will even come to the ground and scavenge the sand on the beaches for crabs.

A pair of scarlet macaws, beautiful birds with brightly feathered wings of yellow, green, blue, and red, squawked grumpily at each other as they feasted on tender green almonds and returned to the task of building their nests in the top of a broken *Cecropia* tree.

Scarlet macaws may sound as if they fuss at each other often, but when they find the right partner, they are inseparable for life!

In the cool, dense jungle shadows, there lay a young mother ocelot with her twin cubs. She watched over them protectively as they playfully wrestled, stalked, and pounced on each other in fun.

In Costa Rica there are six different species of cats, jaguars, pumas, ocelots, margays, and oncillas.

Here on the Osa, the lush green of the jungle touched the blue sweet waters of the Golfo Dulce. All these exotic sights, sounds, and sweet aromas combined and created an enchanting tropical paradise.

And hidden high above, watching the world below with wide-eyed lazy fascination, a tiny, baby two-toed sloth pup clung gently to his mother, yawning widely as he slowly stretched.

A baby sloth is called a pup. Sometimes called Hoffmann's two-toed sloth, they are less common than three-toed sloths, but both types have three toes on their back legs.

CHAPTER

2

A Precious Christmas Gift

All things were *Pura Vida* on this warm sunny morning for the creatures of the jungle.

 Pura Vida is the adopted motto of Costa Rica; it means "pure life" in Spanish.

The baby sloth was born early Christmas morning and was now nearly four weeks old. He clung tightly to his mother as he nursed, nestled safe and secure on top of her soft, furry belly. The mama sloth hung from a branch with her back resting on another limb below her. She hung effortlessly upside down the way sloths do, sticking her tongue out as she yawned lazily and slowly reached for a tender leaf.

 Sloths hang upside down with little effort as their hands naturally clench tight when relaxed.

This tiny sloth pup was now old enough that his mother had begun teaching her baby survival skills to live in the forest. He had begun making short ventures on his own, but always under Mom's watchful gaze. She showed her baby the leaves, buds, and tender shoots that were good to eat.

 Female sloths may give birth to one baby a year, and they will remain together for up to six months or longer, with the mother nursing and teaching the pup how to thrive in the dense Costa Rican treetops.

Blissfully unaware of a faraway tropical storm, the two sloths moved slowly from tree to tree. Today's lesson was how to travel unseen, slowly, and safely through a dense jungle canopy, without ever going to the ground. The mother avoided the smaller, weak, and dead branches that would not support her weight. One misstep could send them both falling to the ground far below. The jungle floor was dangerous for a slow-moving sloth.

The sloth's light-colored fur and slow movements make them hard to spot in the treetops. Sloths rarely go onto the ground, but they do go down to potty—just once a week! On the ground, sloths are more vulnerable to predators like jaguars, domestic dogs, and humans who might capture baby sloths and sell them illegally as pets. Other predators for sloths include snakes, owls, and the endangered giant harpy eagles. Sloths need dense, interconnected rainforest trees to survive and thrive. These tall trees allow sloths, monkeys, and other animals to move unseen and safe while gathering food. Any loss of habitat leads to wider-spaced open areas and a thinning treetop canopy, making it increasingly more difficult for them to travel to distant areas to forage or find a mate.

CHAPTER

3

Paradise in Peril

Every year, humans clear and destroy more and more rainforests. They cut down huge, rare, old-growth trees for their valuable woods, as they clear the land to build houses, plant crops, or raise farm animals like cattle, sheep, and pigs. For sloths, searching for new areas to forage it was increasingly more difficult and dangerous than ever. But the mother sloth remembered a special grove of trees by a distant creek that should be blooming now with tender buds and leaves. She had traveled there many times in the past with her own mother, the first time more than six years ago. It was somewhat far from them, but if their progress was not slowed, they would make it there before dark.

They traveled easily all morning long, and she knew they should be getting close. First, they would reach the jungle creek flowing clear and cold from the distant mountains just beyond the grove of trees she sought. But an hour later, and to her dismay, they came to an open clearing in the forest that had not been there before. The year before, when she made the trip alone the clearing was dense with tall trees and easy to travel. Now all she saw here were the burnt stumps of the giant, ancient trees cut down by loggers. To make matters worse, the humans were still here, below working—and they had dogs!

Between 1940 and 1987, over half of Costa Rican rainforest were cleared. Today, due to conservation measures, it has become a shining example for other counties, almost 60% of the land is once again forested!

But the two sloths remained unseen at the edge of the clearing, safely hidden in the treetops. The mother knew that to get to their grazing area they could not go down to the ground. She would have to find a different path around the wide clearing. It would take much longer for the slow-moving sloths to detour around this unexpected danger to get where they needed to be, and now they might not make it before dark.

To make matters even worse, the sky had begun to darken, and in the distance, lightning flashed, and thunder crashed ever louder. Mother and baby held on tighter as the trees swayed from the strong winds blowing in from the ocean, winds that shook and waved the treetops. Some dead limbs began to break and fall around them. She realized a dangerous tropical storm was coming, and the hungry sloths needed to hurry.

CHAPTER

4

Searching for Sanctuary

The mother urged the baby onto her back, where he would be safer and so they could travel more quickly. The baby sensed her urgency and fear, clutching more tightly to her fur as they set out once again. The day was turning to twilight, so it was too late to turn back now. She had to find them a new path around the man-made clearing, to a safe place to bed down before darkness. There they could weather the approaching tropical storm.

She scrambled faster, as fast she could for a sloth, nervously picking her way along the new trail in the high, unfamiliar treetops. The sky grew ever darker with the swirling storm clouds and gathering nightfall. The wind increased and was now heavy and moist with a driving mist that made it hard to see, as it stung her eyes. She had to hurry now, and she could not be as careful as they moved from limb to limb and tree to tree. They were making progress around the huge clearing in the forest, but it was difficult and slow.

Finally, the clearing was behind them, but larger raindrops had now begun to fall, and then it was if the sky had opened wide to dump buckets of rainwater on the pair of travelers. Soon they were soaked, their thick fur heavy and damp. They shivered as the rain continued to pelt them with a deafening roar.

The forest descended into a wide, steep ravine, and the mother recognized the creek she remembered. Not much further to go now! The stream created a break in the dense jungle canopy, and extra precaution would now be needed. She had crossed this steep, rocky creek that ran swiftly to the ocean many times before, but never at this spot. She was confused because of the new way they had to take around the clearing. She was uncertain where they were, but her instincts told her that they had to cross the dangerous creek here to get to safety.

The mighty trees stretched their canopy across the creek but did not touch. Perhaps they needed to find another spot to cross the rising water. Going to the ground was too dangerous for them, they would have to cross the stream here and now!

Washed Out to Sea!

In desperation, she looked for a way over the creek. Just then a bolt of lightning flashed, and she spotted it! Above them was a possible way across, two long limbs that stretched out to each other from trees on either side of the creek. But would they be too thin and fragile to support them? The limbs barely touched each other above the swirling dark waters cascading below.

The twilight-darkened sky was lit by jagged lightning flashes, she climbed higher, her frightened baby clutching even tighter to her belly. She crawled slowly, carefully further outward, along a thin limb with no leaves that took them over the middle of the raging creek. Finally, she reached the end of the dead, rain-slick branch. Just as she reached out to grab the limb of the next tree, there was a sharp crack, and she reached quickly and grabbed the far branch. She held on with all her might as the branch they were on snapped with a crash and a jolt!

The mother sloth held on to the safety of the new tree, but her baby lost his grip on her wet, moss-covered fur and with an alarming cry fell helplessly toward the flooded creek. She looked down only to see him disappear into the darkness, his cries silenced by the rushing water and thundering storm. Her baby was gone, washed away in the cold, rushing water...

Tropical Dreams

Not far away, safe and dry in their family jungle lodge, a husband and his wife were finishing their dinner as the arriving storm intensified. They and their family had been coming to this winter home on the Osa Peninsula in Costa Rica for many years. Living in Ohio, the couple always looked forward to escaping the cold northern Winter and returning to warm and tropical Costa Rica, their home away from home. From the very start, they both had fallen in love with the unspoiled beauty, and diverse wildlife that surrounded their eco lodge on the edge of the Golfo Dulce.

It was a tropical paradise come true! A youthful dream begun in the many books Dirk read, given to him by his mother June who also had a passion for the tropics. In books like *Call It Courage* and *Kon-Tiki* and in *National Geographic* magazines, he read stories of warm waters, tropical island paradises, bold adventures, and fantastic discoveries far away from his country farm in Ohio. As he read those tales of faraway lands, he would never have believed that one day they would become a reality in his life. Lori, with her passion for nature and adventure, made her the perfect companion to share this tropical paradise with. Together in the Osa rainforest, they lived a simple life, in harmony with nature all around them. No traffic, or modern-day noises here. They were far away from town; their electricity came from the solar panels on the roof of the jungle lodge.

They had both learned the value of nature, how to enjoy it responsibly in harmony. And here in Costa Rica, they worked hard to ready the jungle lodge for their first guest of the season. A family from the United States would be arriving tomorrow. Hosting new guests to their jungle home was rewarding for the couple. It was a way to share and teach others the value of the rainforest and the lessons they had learned from it. The wide-eyed looks of wonder and the many questions from their visitors made them realize and appreciate every day, just how fortunate they were to live here.

This evening, they were treated to a spectacular double rainbow over the ocean that filled the twilight sky before sunset. They kept a wary eye on the approaching storm clouds as they flashed, rumbled, and grew with intensity. After dinner they would ready the jungle lodge, lowering storm shutters and battening down the hatches as Dirks father Bob used to say. To live in such a wild and remote area of the world you had to be prepared, resourceful, and always ready for the unexpected. Soon the storm arrived and ushered in the total darkness of nightfall with brilliant flashes of lightning followed by intense crashes of thunder!

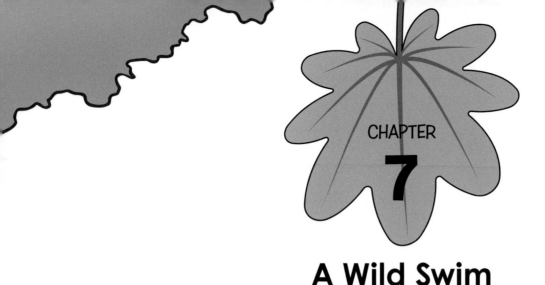

CHAPTER

7

A Wild Swim

The baby sloth was falling through the dark for what seemed an eternity. He landed with a splash into the cold, swift waters of the creek. He was terrified as the rising water carried him in its strong current; it was all he could do just to catch his breath when his head popped above the water. The baby could swim like all sloths, but the strong current swept him downstream, further from the safety of his mother. He had no way of knowing the raging creek was washing him toward the ocean, he was panicked and afraid.

The swirling waters carried him faster now, and the water thundered with a deafening roar. Without warning, he was swept over the edge of a high waterfall, tumbling through the air yet again. He hit the water with a hard splash that took his breath away into a swirling dark pool. The crashing waterfall pushed him under again and again. He popped up, gasping in the cold muddy water. Moving ever faster, he reached out grabbing a vine. The surging creek tugged at the desperate baby, but he hung on for life. Then with a snap, the vine broke and away he went again. The creek bank was wet and slippery, and he could not get out!

He bounced along over the gravel and rocks of the creek bottom, further downstream every second. Suddenly the water spit him out of the jungle and onto a wide rocky beach. He still could not stop, and there was a new sound of thunder. Huge waves crashing, and the raging creek washed him into the warmer storm-tossed waters of the Golfo Dulce. The creek had taken him to the ocean, one he had only seen before in the distance from the safety of the high treetops. The water was deep now, and he could not feel the bottom. He was panicked and struggled to swim, trying to keep his head above the salty, sandy water, but the waves kept taking him underwater.

(Sloths are actually very good swimmers and can swim 3 times faster then they can walk. They can also hold their breath for up to 40 minutes under water!)

Swimming with all his might, he reached the surface and popped up just as a huge wave lifted him high on its crest and sent him crashing and tumbling head over stubby little tail across a rock-strewn beach. There was a strong tug as the receding wave tried to drag him back into the sea. Instinctively, he dug his long sharp claws into the sand and, with all his remaining strength, broke free of the high tide's grip. Now with his last strength, he crawled further up the steep rocky beach, away from the reach of the waves.

The wind blew, the lightning flashed, and rain pelted his back and head. He struggled toward the trees, where he knew he belonged. But where was his mother? In his entire short life, they had never been separated, but she was nowhere to be found. He bumped into a large boulder, it was hard and cold, but it was solid, he would not wash out to sea again. He cried out once more for his mother, but his pitiful squeal was no match for the thunderous storm and crashing waves. It was all too much, he shivered, too weak and afraid to let go, clinging on with all his tiny sloth might to the huge cold boulder. He was beyond exhaustion and sore from bumping into rocks. Holding tightly to the boulder, he closed his eyes and tried his best to shut out the darkness and the fierce storm around him.

CHAPTER 8

Howler Monkey Morning

Morning dawned clear and bright at the jungle lodge, and Lori was up first for the new day. Their sleep had been disturbed long before sunrise with the storm, and now the deafening roar of a howler monkey troop hollering in the tree canopy above their tiny tin-roof casita. They lay in bed, trying to get another hour of sleep. Above them, the monkeys foraged for tender leaves and shoots. Every now and then a dead branch or nut would fall on the metal roof with a startling *bang!* Between the loud monkeys, the crashing of waves, and the rest of the jungle sounds, there would be no more sleeping in this morning!

In truth, they both enjoyed waking up early. Every morning held the possibility of a spectacular new Sunrise. The sun had already begun to peek over the mountains beyond the distant shore of the gulf, and it shined brightly through the bug netting of their tent.

"Wake up, sleepyhead," whispered Lori as she prodded Dirk, "We have a big day ahead of us, our guests are flying in this afternoon!"

Dirk grumbled as he rolled over, putting his pillow over his head to block the sunlight and jungle noise. "Just one more minute, that storm was intense; it kept me up all night," he said in a voice muffled by his pillow.

But Lori was persistent. "Come on," she prodded him. "A morning walk to Tiger Point to watch the sunrise will wake us both up! And you never know what we might discover washed up on the beach after a storm like that."

Dirk knew she was right: they had lots to do today, and Lori was always up for a new adventure. He sat up in bed, stretched and yawned widely. It was then he heard the barks of dogs somewhere on the beach. It was probably their neighbor's dogs running loose again, out looking for trouble and something washed up on the sand. The dogs owners knew letting them run loose in the jungle was a danger to the dogs, and to other small, helpless animals that lived there. Just last month, their friend's little dog was bitten by a poisonous fer-de-lance snake and barely survived.

"Looks like another day in paradise," he said cheerfully. "I'll make some coffee, and hot water for your tea; then let's go for a walk on the beach and take a sunrise swim in the tide pool by Tiger Point." Within minutes they had swimsuits on and with beach towels in hand set out barefoot, walking hand in hand down the beach towards Tiger Point nearly a mile away.

CHAPTER

9

All Alone

The baby sloth awoke in alarm to the screech of parrots in a palm tree outlined by blue skies. He could barely see. Sand and salt burned his eyes, and it was in his nose, ears, and mouth. He had swallowed saltwater too, and he was very thirsty now. And he was alone, still clinging tight to the boulder that had saved his life. He tried to call out for his mother, but the only sound that he made was a pitiful high-pitched squeal. He coughed, clearing his parched throat, and tried calling again. The squeak was louder now, but still a tiny cry compared to the crashing waves. How could his mother find him if she could not hear him?

The tide was much lower now, and what had been a narrow sliver of sand and rocks in the storm last night was now a wide, sand and boulder-strewn beach. He was hidden amongst an area of large rocks, the waves now breaking far away.

Somehow, he had survived the fall into the creek, the cold night swim and the fierce storm unharmed. But now he needed to get off the beach before the sun made it too hot or a predator found him. He would have a long, slow crawl across the sand and rocks to make it to the dense green jungle and its tall trees. There he might find safety. He would climb a tree and be out of the bright sun, it would be cooler, and maybe he would find his mother there to.

He was trying to gather enough courage to let go of the rock. Just as he was about to cry out one more time he heard them, the sound of barking dogs!

They were still in the distance, but the barking got louder as they came down the beach in his direction. He knew dogs were dangerous, his mother had taught him early on. They were one of many other predators sloths needed to be wary of, especially for slow sloths on the ground. But these dogs were still far away, barking at a troop of squirrel monkeys who chattered angrily back at them, safe in the tall palm trees.

He kept quiet, shivering with fear, too terrified to move, and now he could not cry out for help. His only hope was to remain very still and quiet where he was. But what if the dogs caught scent of him in the wind? Their keen sense of smell might detect him. And just one sniff of a sloth stranded on the beach would lead them right to his hiding place. If only he were older and bigger, with sharp sloth claws, he might be able to defend himself, but he was only a helpless baby. The dogs walked side by side, leaving deep footprints in the soft sand of the beach. Soon they would reach the boulders where the baby sloth was barely hidden from view.

(Sloths rely on their camouflage to protect themselves from predators. However, when threatened an adult sloth can use its long claws and sharp teeth to defend themselves. Despite their slow movements sloths are very strong.)

Tiger Point Rescue

Dirk and Lori walked onto the beach, and they soon noticed two sets of dog prints side by side in the soft sand. The tracks were going the same direction they were, toward Tiger Point. The beach curved, and they heard barking but could not yet see the dogs.

"I bet that's our neighbor's two dogs barking at monkeys again," said Lori as they jumped from rock to rock, carefully crossing a swollen muddy creek flowing across the beach into the ocean. Its brown water had been higher during the storm, carrying large branches and debris as it spread out into the clear blue water of the bay. There was floating driftwood near the shore washed out of the creek, some was tossed back onto the beach by the waves. They liked to collect the interesting twisted, dead pieces of wood, shells, and other items from their morning walks to make wind mobiles and decorations for the jungle lodge.

As they rounded the curved beach, they saw the dogs in the distance near the point of land named Punta Tigre

 (Tiger Point, named for the pride of pumas that locals say once lived there long ago).

"I don't think it's monkeys they are barking at; look, they're barking towards the rocks by the water, not the trees in the jungle," Dirk said. "Let's hurry and see what's going on!"

They began trotting now, their bare feet kicking up sand behind them. They were now closer to the dogs, they barked furiously at something within the pile of boulders.

"That's strange," said Lori. "What could it be? Something was there, washed up by the storm."

The dogs continued barking and did not even notice the humans approaching them. What was it clinging to the other side of a large boulder, partially hidden from their sight.

"Hurry," said Dirk. "I think the dogs found a live animal, and they might harm it."

He reached down and picked up a stick and ran toward the dogs, yelling! The animals stopped barking and turned in surprise. With one last look at their would-be prey in the rocks, they turned and quickly scampered with their tails between their legs, into the jungle.

CHAPTER

11

A Furry Discovery

Lori caught up with Dirk. "We made it here just in time," said Lori, panting. They were both out of breath.

Slowly they approached the boulder. A small, dark grey, furry looking creature could be seen clinging to it.

"Yes," agreed Dirk. "Whatever it is, I think the dogs wanted it for breakfast!"

He spoke softly to the furry object, and it stirred. "Hey there, little one, are you okay?"

The wet furry creature raised its tiny head and let out a frail, frightened, squeaky cry. It seemed to sense the kindness in the human voices and looked at the two of them, then cried out again.

"Oh my," exclaimed Lori, "it's a baby sloth! How did it end up here?"

"A beach is no place for a tiny sloth," said Dirk. "Look at the front claws. It's a two-toed sloth and much too young to be here all alone."

"Maybe it was lost from its mother in that terrible storm last night," said Lori. "That's why he is crying for her."

"Let's check to see if she's still somewhere nearby in the trees," said Dirk.

Again and again, the baby cried out as the two rescuers looked around and searched the trees along the beach carefully for the mother sloth. They listened closely for a mother sloth's whistle reply to her baby but heard none. Only a loud screech from a large black hawk watched them intently from his perch high in a palm tree above the beach.

"You won't get this little sloth either," Dirk shouted at the hawk. It seemed to understand, turned, and quickly flew away, disappearing into the forest.

"Aww, look at him," said Lori. "The poor little thing must have spent the whole night here in the storm."

"That muddy creek we crossed was flooded from all the rain," said Dirk.

"He could have fallen from a tree into the fast water, then washed up here," replied Lori. "He will not survive here on the beach in the hot sun, and his mother is nowhere to be seen. We can't leave him here."

Dirk said, "Let's take him back to the jungle lodge and rinse the sand and saltwater from his eyes and mouth. Then we can call the animal rescue center, and they will know what to do."

"Yes," said Lori. "They will take good care of him and maybe even find him a foster mother."

Dirk slowly removed the towel from his shoulder and spoke with a soft and soothing voice to the baby who was shivering with cold and crying out in fright. "It's okay, little one, you're safe now. Let's get you off this beach and out of the sun."

He reached down and gently placed the beach towel around the baby and began to lift. The tiny sloth held firmly to the rock and didn't budge, his strong muscles and long, sharp claws digging into the boulder, holding on tighter. Who could blame him? This boulder he had found in the dark during the storm had kept him safe all night.

Lori spoke softly again to the frightened baby. "It's okay, little fella, we won't harm you." She said with a soothing voice. Then Dirk gently but firmly grasped the baby and with a quick tug, pulled him off the rock. Into Dirk's arms he went with a frightened whimper.

"Let's hurry!" urged Lori, "it's getting hot here on the open beach. He needs shade, a cool rinse, and some fresh drinking water. He must be so thirsty."

They gave one final look in the nearby trees but still saw no sign of the mother; then they set off quickly down the beach. The bundled baby sloth squirmed and wiggled anxiously in the towel but cried out less now, surrendering his fate to his kind human rescuers.

CHAPTER

12

Safe at Last

Soon they were back to the cool shade of the almond trees surrounding the jungle lodge. The cry of the jungle baby alerted Carlos and María, their workers at the jungle lodge. Carlos had grown up living near the jungle all his life and knew much about the native plants and animals there. Dirk had learned much from Carlos and his Costa Rica family.

"Perezoso bambino," said Carlos.

(Perezoso is the Spanish name for sloths, meaning lazy.)

"It looks so tiny and scared!" added María with a concerned look.

Dirk and Lori told them how they had found the baby and chased dogs away just in time.

"We should take him to the nearby animal sanctuary and have it checked out as soon as possible," said Lori.

Yes, agreed Carlos. "Without his mother, he is too young to survive in the jungle alone. You were wise to rescue him from the beach."

Dirk carried the baby over to a freshwater spigot and began gently rinsing the salt and sand off him. The sloth squirmed and cried out in alarm when the cold water was poured over his face and eyes.

"Perhaps he thinks he is back in the ocean," said María. She handed a plastic cup to Lori. "Use this and pour the water slowly, and he might not be so frightened."

Dirk poured some fresh cool water into his hand and held it near the baby's mouth. The tiny sloth sniffed the water and then began lapping it up in tiny mouthfuls with his thirsty tongue. He was so thirsty from swallowing the ocean salt water. Lori used the cup to slowly rinse the baby. After two handfuls of water and a gentle rinse, they were able to remove most of the salt and sand from the baby's face and matted fur.

"Look," said Lori, "he seems much happier now!"

Indeed, the baby was looking up at the rescuers and seemed to be grinning at them.

"Now let's take him to the Serenity Wildlife Sanctuary," said Dirk. "They have trained people there who will know how to feed and care for him."

"Okay," said Lori, "but we should give him a name first. Maybe we can name him Guanabana after our property? After all, he was found near here."

"That's a mouthful of a name," laughed Dirk, "but Guanabana it is! Now let's dry him off and get him in the truck right away; the rescue center is just down the road."

The jungle lodge was built on land that had many years ago been a plantation of Guanabana fruit trees, a delicious, large spiked looking fruit that grew on the trees there. Now after many years the jungle had slowly taken the property back over. This was much better for the animals to have many different plants and trees then just a single crop.

(Guanabanas are sometimes called Soursop, they taste like a blend of mangos, pineapples, and bananas. It is high in vitamin C and helps strengthen your immune system.)

CHAPTER 13

Serenity Wildlife Sanctuary

Years ago, a wealthy, mysterious man named Mr. Hughes had purchased thousands of acres of pasture and farmlands that had been old-growth rainforest years ago. But the land had been cleared of trees, which were sold. The farmers then used the open land to plant crops and graze livestock. This was not good for the forest animals, who lost their homes, food source, and with no trees, their safe jungle pathways.

Who was this man, and why was he buying up so much land the locals wondered. Some said there were rumors he might create a resort and open a luxury hotel there, maybe even a golf course. Soon there was much activity; a lake was dug, trees were planted, and many jobs were created. Experts were brought in, and many studies were conducted.

The man was using his wealth wisely for conservation, employing biologists, botanists, and local workers to restore the rainforest to help heal the earth. He and his wife were conservationists at heart and were doing what they could to undo some of the harm humans had caused to the rainforest. Workers planted many acres of native plants and trees to replace the open pastures. Replanting the rainforest helped fill in the missing green patches of jungle that remained. Now animals could once again travel among the treetops of the dense forest it created, restoring their high protective pathways. It was a very good thing he was doing for the land on the Osa peninsula, agreed all the people, and he fittingly named the property Serenity. Mr. Hughes had done this before in Africa, there too creating huge preserves which saved threatened animals such as elephants, lions, and rhinos.

At Serenity they also created a rescue area where injured, displaced, and orphaned animals could recover and be cared for until they were healthy or old enough to be released back into the wild. They had helped all sorts of animals there and before long, people from all over Costa Rica knew to bring them to Serenity. Scarlet macaws, howler monkeys, anteaters, wild pigs called peccaries, and orphaned jungle cats—pumas, jaguars, and spotted ocelots—were all taken care of by kind workers who gave them love, food, and the medicines they needed to get better. It was here that Dirk and Lori would bring the little orphaned sloth they had named Guanabana.

CHAPTER
14

Special Delivery

They placed baby Guanabana in a small cardboard box with a clean towel as a security blanket and set off for Serenity Wildlife Sanctuary. Lori drove the truck, and Dirk held the box with the precious sloth in his lap. The gravel road was very bumpy, and Lori drove slowly and carefully to avoid jostling scared little Guanabana to much.

When the vehicle hit a bump, he cried out in alarm, grasping the edge of the box with his strong claws. "It's okay, little one," said Dirk in a soft, soothing voice; "we will be there soon."

Guanabana was calmer now and looked up at the kind man with a tiny sloth smile.

"I wish we could keep and take care of you ourselves," Dirk whispered loud enough for Lori to hear. But they both knew the people at Serenity Wildlife Sanctuary would know what is best for an orphaned baby sloth.

Soon they arrived at the entrance to the animal rescue. They parked in front of a huge metal gate, and Lori turned off the truck.

"How will they know we are here?" Lori wondered out loud.

"Up there," Dirk pointed. "They will see us on that security camera. Let's get out and hold Guanabana up for them to see."

In the Serenity security building a woman looked up at the monitor when the gate alarm sounded. A blue pickup truck she had seen on the road before had now stopped in front of the entrance gate. A man and a woman were getting out, and he was carrying a small cardboard box and walking toward the camera.

"What is going on here?" she said to a man sitting beside her.

The man looked over her shoulder at the security monitor. "It appears they have an animal in that box," he replied.

Together they watched as the couple approached the camera and were astonished to see a small furry animal looking at them. Then to their surprise, the creature let out a loud, pitiful cry.

"Hello," said the guard into the microphone, "what do you have there?"

Dirk and Lori were startled and jumped at the loud, unseen voice coming from the speaker.

"It's a baby sloth we found washed up on the beach this morning. There was no sign of his mother, and he is hungry. Would you please let someone at the animal sanctuary know we are here and that it needs help?" pleaded Dirk.

"Of course," said the guard, his voice friendlier now. "Stay where you are, and I will notify someone right away."

15

An Angel for Animals

They waited at the gate for just a few minutes. Soon a young woman in a small cart drove up on the opposite side of the huge gate as it slowly began to open.

"Hello," she said with concern, "my name is Aida, I am the director of the Serenity rescue facility. The guards tell me you found a baby sloth." She peered into the box and smiled warmly at the helpless tiny creature, Guanabana looked up at Aida and gave a soft, timid squeak.

"Yes, we found him on our beach this morning," Dirk said. "He was clinging to a boulder in the storm all night long. We searched around the area but could see no sign of its mother."

Guanabana squeaked once more as Dirk held the box closer for Aida to see.

"Aww, it is so young and tiny," she said. "You were wise to bring it here to us. Some people try to keep them illegally as pets, and they have a very special diet. We will of course take him in and give him a good checkup to make sure he is not injured. When he gets bigger, we can release him back into the jungle.

"Please follow me," she said eagerly. "My staff will see him right away!"

They followed her cart into the compound, past a huge greenhouse filled with a variety of native plants of all sizes. They passed a large lake, and many groves of plantains. Then they came upon workers busy trimming mango and almond trees. Soon they arrived at the rescue center. Dirk and Lori looked around at the cages, which contained injured and orphaned animals, monkeys and macaws, an ocelot, an anteater, and more. Two workers were waiting for them.

As Lori handed them the box with the baby, she smiled and told them, "We named him Guanabana, and we know you will take good care of him."

Aida then gave them a tour of the other rescue center facilities and explained Serenity's program to them.

"Our experts and local workers help to replant forest with the right plants and trees. In this way, we create the right habitat so we can repopulate the native cat species like the ocelots, jaguars, and pumas. All this to help restore the balance of nature and wildlife on the Osa Peninsula."

Serenity, as they learned, was much more than just an animal rescue center. It was a shining example of how humans could help heal and restore the rainforest, giving back to nature.

Sweet Goodbye

When it was time to leave, Dirk and Lori said goodbye to the baby sloth.

"Don't be afraid, little one," said Lori. "They will take good care of you, and we will be back to visit".

They thanked Aida and the sanctuary workers for their wonderful work with the animals.

"Please tell Mr. Hughes we truly appreciate what he is doing here," said Dirk. "He is a friend of the Osa and all things wild!"

"Yes," said Aida, "I will be sure to let him know. He is a kind and generous man. We will give Guanabana the best of care and, if we are lucky, perhaps find him a foster mother to teach him how to live in the rainforest.

"Please come back and you can check on Guanabana's progress," she said. "I promise I will give you updates. Perhaps he will be ready to release by then."

Together the couple drove back to the jungle lodge. What an exciting morning it had been for them! Their hearts were filled with happiness for having had the opportunity to help such a beautiful, helpless creature, who had survived a storm and a long, scary night.

"I believe things happen for a reason," said Dirk. "Maybe it's to share this story with people. There's certainly a special lesson here for everyone. Perhaps people alone may not change the world, but many people working together can make a huge difference. We all need to do just one kind thing for the planet every day. What a wonderful improvement that would make for our earth and all living things!"

Later that very same evening they sat on the beach, watching the brilliant stars over the Golfo Dulce. The first full moon of the new year cast a silver glow over both land and calm sea. They chatted quietly about the extraordinary day they had experienced. Just then a brilliant shooting star streaked across the huge night sky.

"Quick," said Lori, "make a wish!"

"My wish already came true," said Dirk." And he reached and held Lori's hand in the moonlight.

"And how fortunate for Guanabana that we came along when we did! I believe there are no ordinary days," said Lori, "when we look for ways to make each day special."

"Yes," agreed Dirk, "Guanabana was one lucky little sloth and so are we!"

By the light of candles and the moon's soft glow, they began to write down the story of what happened this day, to share with others: the story of Guanabana, the lucky little sloth!

The End (?)

CHAPTER

17

A Final Farewell

As the days passed Aida called from time to time, giving them updates on Guanabana's progress. To give him the best nutrition, they flew a worker to Florida to buy an expensive baby sloth formula made there. It was necessary to feed the hungry sloth up to eight times night and day. Dirk and Lori were allowed to stop by and visit the sanctuary. They took turns feeding the ever-growing baby sloth with a bottle. It was during the second visit they got exciting news when Aida told them it was discovered Guanabana was not a little boy as they had assumed, she was indeed a girl!

Under Aida and the Serenity staff's gentle care, Guanabana thrived and gained almost two pounds in the first week. Then early one morning a Tranquility driver stopped by the jungle lodge and said that Aida had asked for them to come right away to Serenity.

"Oh no," said Dirk with concern. "Is Guanabana okay?"

"Do not be alarmed," the man replied, smiling. "Everything is fine, but she said to hurry!"

They left quickly and following the driver to the rescue center.

"What could this possibly mean," asked Lori with concern.

"That man said everything was okay. Perhaps little Guanabana is going to be released today," suggested Dirk.

"But isn't she too young to live in the jungle alone?" said Lori.

"We will soon find out," said Dirk.

As the couple pulled into the sanctuary and got out of the truck, Aida, with two of her coworkers were waiting in front of the open enclosure which had been Guanabana's home for the past two months.

"Hello," said Dirk. "We came as soon as we could. What's going on with Guanabana?"

"Is everything okay?" asked Lori.

Then they heard the baby sloth cry out as she had done on the beach the day they found her. But it was a happy sound now.

Aida smiled assuredly and pointed into the tree just above the enclosure. They looked up and searched the branches. To their amazement, hanging upside down on a limb above was a large, grey, furry two-toed sloth.

"It is an adult female," said Aida. "She appeared here overnight, coming to the call of the baby. One of the workers heard her calling back out to the baby early this morning."

Guanabana then let out another cry to the larger sloth, who answered in a low, friendly whistle.

"Could this sloth be its mother?" Lori asked.

"It is very possible," said Aida. "Your property is less than two miles away, and she has had two months to search for Guanabana. Sloths have excellent hearing, and she may have finally found her! I wanted you both to be here to see them meet. You two were responsible for rescuing her from the beach, and so you should be here as she returns to the wild, where sloths belong."

Aida then handed Dirk a pair of long-sleeve leather gloves with which to pick up the baby. "As you already know, it's important that we not handle her with our bare hands," she said.

She then unlocked the cage door, and Dirk reached inside and gently picked up Guanabana. He carefully carried her out of the enclosure and placed her in a low branch of the tree the female was on.

"Now let's see if she comes down to accept her," said Aida hopefully.

Little Guanabana squealed anxiously as Dirk lifted her up to the tree limb. The female slowly looked their way but did not move. Everyone held their breath and watched to see what would happen. Then the mother sloth slowly began to creep down the tree. The baby looked up and crawled upward.

"She is coming down," said Lori with quiet excitement in her voice.

Together they and the workers watched with hopeful anticipation as the two sloths climbed slowly toward one another, Guanabana climbing up the tree, the larger sloth coming down. It seemed an eternity until at last they met, touching their pink sloth noses together. They sniffed and made soft, quiet, cooing sounds between themselves that could barely be heard from the ground.

Then magically, it happened. The larger female sloth slowly reached out to little Guanabana, gently pulling the baby to her. The humans on the ground watched in amazement as Guanabana gave her a tender lick on the tip of her nose and then, with a squeak of excitement, eagerly climbed onto the larger sloth, embracing her in a loving sloth hug.

"It appears she will accept Guanabana as her baby," Aida said with relief.

And they watched, as together both animals took one long last look back down to the kind humans on the ground as if to say thank you and goodbye. Then, silently and ever so slowly, they climbed up the tree, into the safety and freedom of the rainforest.

"Guanabana is home again and will be safe," said Aida, smiling.

Together they watched through tears of happiness as the two sloths climbed higher and higher into the trees until they slowly disappeared, blending into the dense jungle canopy above.

Dirk turned to Lori and gave her a reassuring hug. "Let's go home now" he whispered softly.

"That lucky little sloth has at last found a mother. Yes," Lori added, smiling, "and we are so lucky to have found sweet little Guanabana. She will remain in our hearts forever!"

Pura Vida! The End

Morgan's Jungle Lodge

Sunrise over Golfe Dolce

Authors Dirk and Lori Morgan

Lucky Little Sloth

Guanabana clinging to safety

Rescue at Tiger Point

Rinsing Guanabana off

Guanabana headed to Rescue Center

Guanabana safe at last

Lori, Dirk, Aida and Guanabana

Lori, Aida, Dirk at Rescue Center

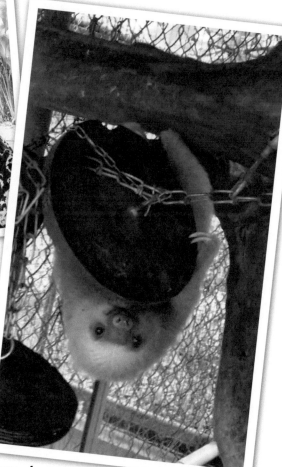

Guanabana playing at Rescue Center

Release Day for Guanabana

Happily Ever After!

"Authors, Dirk and Lori Morgan with Lana Wedmore center founder of the White Hawk Foundation and author of her own autobiography, "Married to Paradise"."

Most people will never have the chance to find a baby sloth abandoned on the beach, but everyone can help all the Rainforest animals by supporting the White Hawk Foundation.

Pura Vida, Dirk and Lori Morgan

HELP SAVE THE COSTA RICAN RAINFOREST which contains 2.5 % of all of the world's biodiversity--animals, flora and fauna--by contributing to the White Hawk Foundation, a USA registered 501(c)3 non-profit whose mission is to buy and preserve land into perpetuity.

Please scan this QR code to donate.

Printed in the United States
by Baker & Taylor Publisher Services